Native Americans Make History

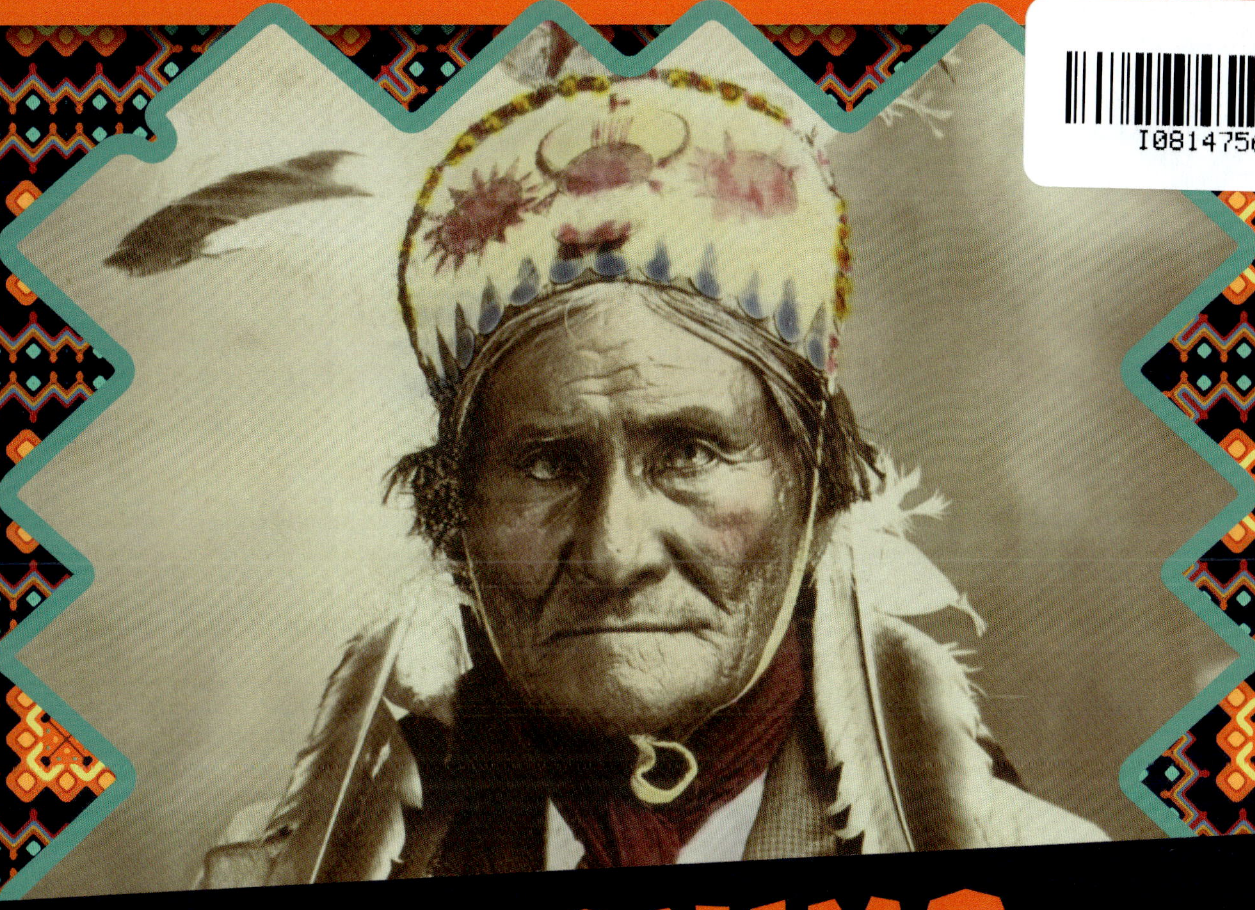

GERONIMO

Enslow PUBLISHING

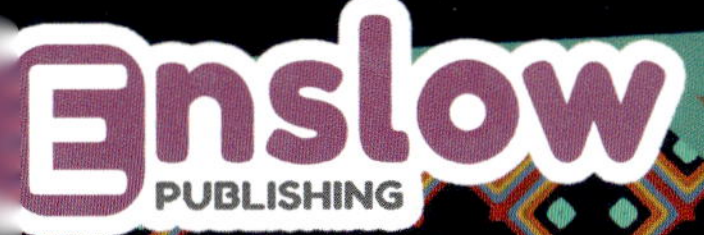

INVESTIGATE!

Abby Badach Doyle

Please visit our website, www.enslow.com. For a free color catalog of all our high-quality books, call toll free 1-800-398-2504 or fax 1-877-980-4454.

Library of Congress Cataloging-in-Publication Data
Names: Doyle, Abby Badach, author.
Title: Geronimo / Abby Badach Doyle.
Description: New York : Enslow Publishing, [2023] | Series: Native Americans make history | Includes bibliographical references and index.
Identifiers: LCCN 2021051923 (print) | LCCN 2021051924 (ebook) | ISBN 9781978527645 (library binding) | ISBN 9781978527621 (paperback) | ISBN 9781978527638 (set) | ISBN 9781978527652 (ebook)
Subjects: LCSH: Geronimo, 1829-1909–Juvenile literature. | Apache Indians–Kings and rulers–Biography–Juvenile literature. | Apache Indians–Wars–Juvenile literature.
Classification: LCC E99.A6 D69 2023 (print) | LCC E99.A6 (ebook) | DDC 979.004/97250092–dc23/eng/20211022
LC record available at https://lccn.loc.gov/2021051923
LC ebook record available at https://lccn.loc.gov/2021051924

Portions of this work were originally authored by Heather Moore Niver and published as *The Life of Geronimo*. All new material in this edition is authored by Abby Badach Doyle.

Published in 2023 by
Enslow Publishing
29 E. 21st Street
New York, NY 10010

Designer: Leslie Taylor
Editor: Abby Badach Doyle

Photo credits: Cover background Dmitriy NDM/Shutterstock.com; cover image (portrait), pp. 5, 17 Everett Collection/Shutterstock.com; series background (cover and interior, Native American pattern) Dmitriy NDM/Shutterstock.com; series artwork Nevada31/Shutterstock.com; p. 5 (logo) https://commons.wikimedia.org/wiki/File:501-Parachute-Infantry-Regiment.svg; p. 5 (stamp) neftali/Shutterstock.com; p. 5 https://commons.wikimedia.org/wiki/File:Flickr_-_The_U.S._Army_-_JUMP%5E_XVIII_Airborne_Corps.jpg; p. 7 (engraving) Old Paper Studios/Alamy.com; p. 7 (harvest) Zhukova_Anastasia/Shutterstock.com; p. 7 (map) stas11/Shutterstock.com; p. 9 (mustangs) Daniel Eskridge/Shutterstock.com; p. 9 (family) H. H. Clarke/LOC.gov; p. 11 https://commons.wikimedia.org/wiki/File:Apache_chieff_Geronimo_(right)_and_his_warriors_in_1886.jpg; p. 13 (silo art) Cattallina/Shutterstock.com; p. 13 (silo figure) shaineast/Shutterstock.com; p. 13 (engraving) Frederick sic Remington/LOC.gov; p. 15 (teepee) Hammon Photography/Shutterstock.com; p. 15 https://commons.wikimedia.org/wiki/File:Gadsden_Purchase_Cities.svg; p. 17 (reservation) K. T. Dodge (Katherine Taylor)/LOC.gov; p. 19 https://commons.wikimedia.org/wiki/File:San_Carlos_Apache_Reservation_-_panoramio.jpg; p. 19 (Clum) https://commons.wikimedia.org/wiki/File:Clum-horseback-alaska.jpg; p. 21 C. S. Fly (1886)/LOC.gov; p. 23 C. S. Fly/LOC.com; p. 25 (portrait) National Photo Company Collection/LOC.gov; p. 25 (family) https://commons.wikimedia.org/wiki/File:Ta-ayz-slath,_wife_of_Geronimo,_and_one_child_restored.jpg; p. 27 (group) Geronimo and Apaches at the St. Louis Fair. United States Saint Louis Missouri, 1904. Photograph. https://www.loc.gov/item/99471922/.; p. 27 (car) https://commons.wikimedia.org/wiki/File:Geronimo_in_a_1905_Locomobile_Model_C.jpg; p. 27 (parade) Keystone View Company/LOC.gov; p. 29 (in field) https://commons.wikimedia.org/wiki/File:Geronimo,_biographer,_and_translator.png; p. 29 (grave) Carol M. Highsmith/LOC.gov.

Printed in the United States of America

CPSIA compliance information: Batch #CSENS23: For further information contact Enslow Publishing, New York, New York, at 1-800-398-2504.

CONTENTS

Words in the glossary appear in **bold** type the first time they are used in the text.

GERONIMO!

Geronimo was a fearless Apache warrior and a strong leader. He was known as the last Native American leader to surrender, or peacefully give up, to the U.S. government. Before that, he spent many years avoiding capture.

Geronimo became very famous. He even sold signed items and photos of himself, like **celebrities** do today. There are many TV shows and movies about Geronimo. However, his real life was rich with stories beyond the battles he fought. Geronimo was also a medicine man, which is a special kind of healer and leader of his people.

Geronimo's Apache name was Goyahkla, which means "One Who Yawns."

The 501st Infantry Regiment, a group of soldiers in the U.S. Army, is named after Geronimo.

Explore More!

Why do people yell "Geronimo!" when they jump? In the 1940s, the U.S. Army asked soldiers to shout their names during **parachute** drills. One man, Aubrey Eberhardt, had just watched a movie about Geronimo. He yelled that instead to be funny. It stuck!

A PEACEFUL CHILDHOOD

Geronimo was born on June 16, 1829, in No-Doyohn Canyon, Mexico. Today, that land is located in Arizona. He belonged to the Bedonkohe band of the Chiricahua Apache Tribe.

Geronimo and his family were farmers. As a boy, he learned to grow crops like corn, beans, and pumpkins. Geronimo would play and hunt with the other boys. They learned how to ride horses and make bows and arrows. It was a peaceful time. However, by the time he became an adult, Geronimo's people were at war with the Mexican and U.S. governments.

Geronimo's family were farmers. They also traded goods with other tribes.

Western Plains American Indian trading post

Explore More!

The Apache are North American Native Americans. They lived in what is now Mexico and the Southwest United States. In Geronimo's time, they grew crops, but also moved around to hunt animals and gather wild food. They also traded with other tribes and villages.

LOVE AND LOSS

In 1846, Geronimo was 17 years old. He joined Apache warriors on raids, or sudden attacks, on neighboring tribes. Apache leaders asked him to join the **council** of warriors. The invitation let him join his tribe on the warpath. Geronimo saw this as a great honor.

Geronimo had loved an Apache woman named Alope for a long time. As a warrior, now he could marry her. They got married and moved to a new tepee near where Geronimo's mother lived. Alope decorated it with beads and paintings on animal hide.

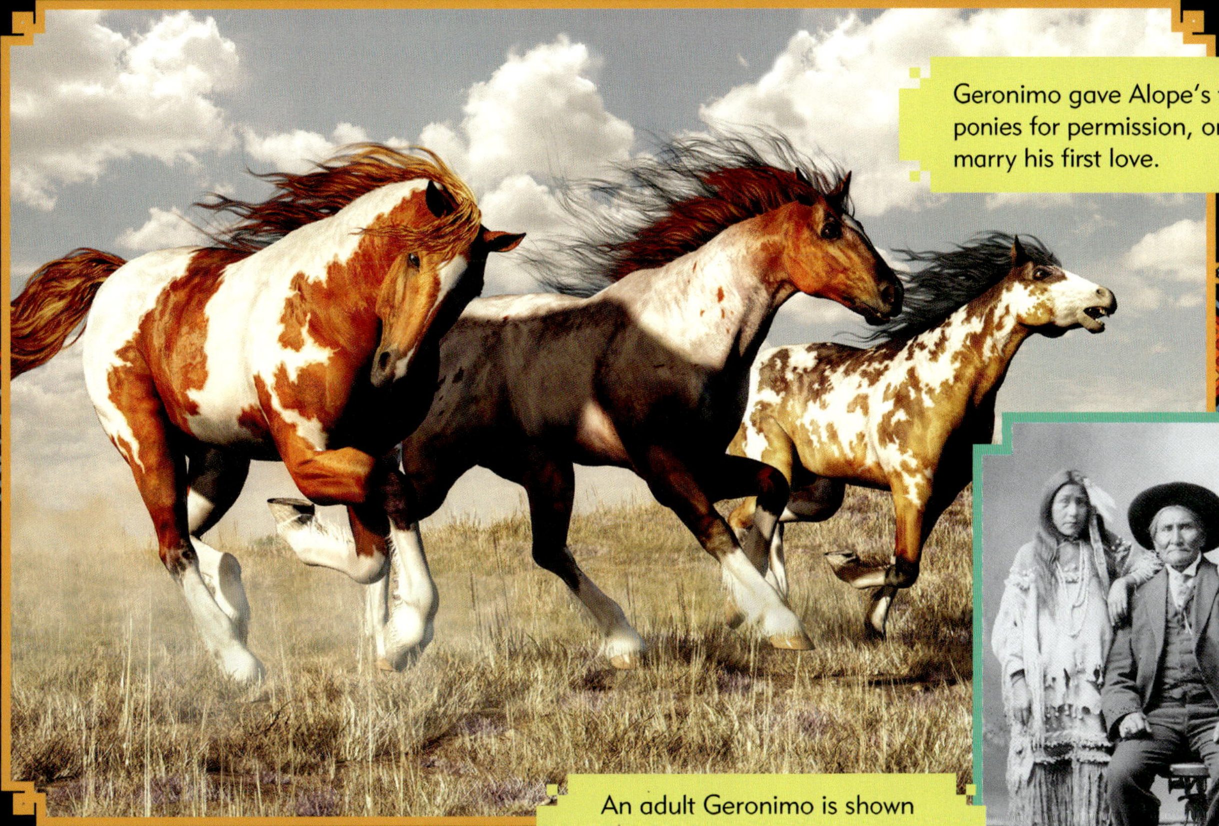

Geronimo gave Alope's father many ponies for permission, or consent, to marry his first love.

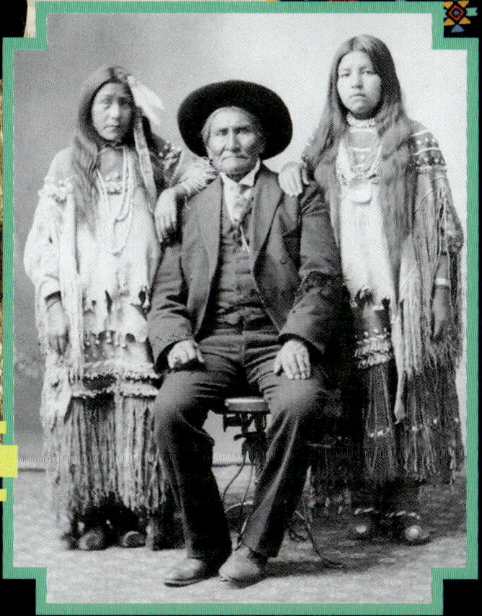

An adult Geronimo is shown here with two of his nieces.

Geronimo was known to love his family. Geronimo's father died when Geronimo was a small boy. Geronimo took care of his mother, who never married again. As a father, Geronimo enjoyed watching his children play in nature like he did.

Together, Geronimo and Alope had three children. They lived a happy life. Around 1858, Geronimo's tribe traveled south to an area near Janos, Mexico. They made a camp outside the city.

One day while Geronimo and others were in the city to trade, Mexican soldiers raided their camp and killed Geronimo's aging mother, wife, and children. Other women and children of the tribe were killed too. Geronimo was sick with sadness. He set his family's belongings on fire. This was an Apache practice after someone died. Then, Geronimo rode alone into the **wilderness**.

Geronimo (far right) stands with his band, or small local group. He said about the raid by Mexican soldiers, "I had lost all."

Explore More!

Geronimo's life changed after this event. He swore he would get back at those who killed his family and his people. Geronimo became a leader of the Chiricahua Apache. He led Apache warriors in battles and raids against their enemies.

A VOICE IN THE WILD

While alone in the wilderness, stories say Geronimo heard a voice. It said, "No gun can ever kill you. I will take the bullets from the guns of the Mexicans, so they will have nothing but powder. And I will guide your arrows." This gave Geronimo the courage, or bravery, to fight.

In a later battle, he fought with great strength. Some say the Mexicans called out "Geronimo!" This might have been a call to the **Catholic** Saint Jerome for help. Around this time, he became known by that name.

In this drawing, Geronimo leads his band back from a raid in Mexico.

Explore More!

Geronimo gathered a group of 200 men to help him hunt down the Mexican soldiers who killed his family. Geronimo had a **violent** style of fighting. He and his band of warriors would seek **revenge** against Mexico for the next 10 years.

A NEW ENEMY

Geronimo and the Apache had fought the Mexicans for years. But when United States settlers came west, they had a new enemy.

The **Mexican-American War** ended in 1848. The two countries signed a treaty, or peace agreement. In it, Mexico gave land to the United States, including the land where Geronimo's people lived. The Apache had called this land home for centuries. When the American settlers came, they limited where Apache people could live and hunt. With their **traditional** ways of life at risk, the Apache began to stand up for themselves.

traditional Native American tepee

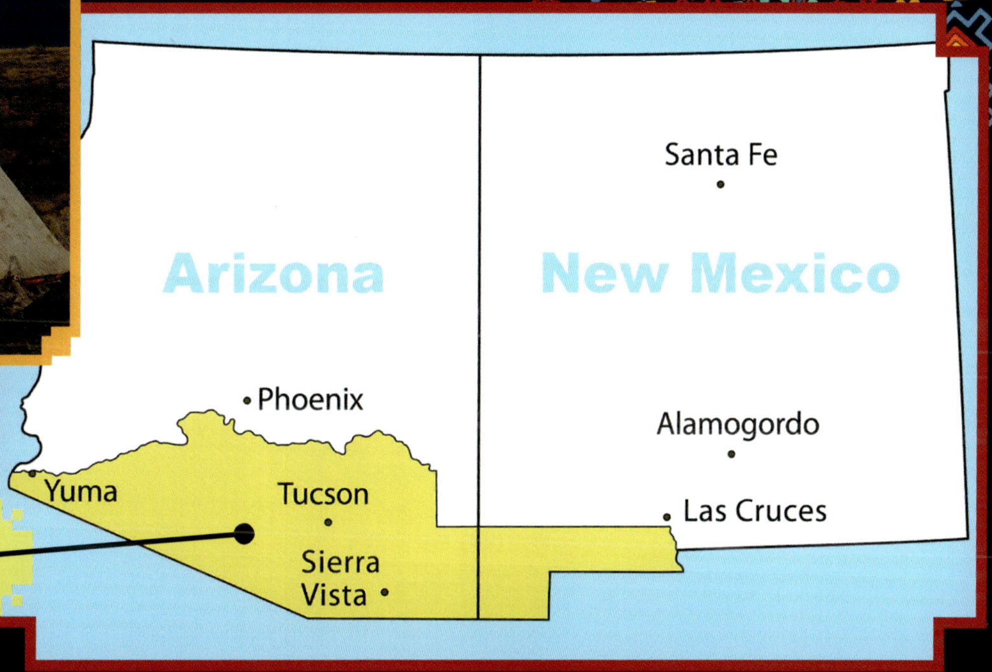

The 1853 land deal is known as the Gadsden Purchase.

Explore More!

In 1853, the United States government paid Mexico $10 million for even more land, now part of Arizona and New Mexico. Settlers built ranches, homes, and mines. They made it clear they thought they owned Apache land.

FORCED TO MOVE

Soon, settlers flooded the Southwest to dig for gold. The Apache would ambush, or surprise attack, the settlers' wagons. War and raids lasted for many years. The Apache leader at the time, Cochise, was a respected chief. After years of battle, he wanted peace.

In 1872, Cochise agreed to the creation of a reservation for his people. A reservation is land set aside by the U.S. government for Native Americans to live. Geronimo disagreed with this. He was deeply saddened when the Apache could no longer roam, or wander, free.

As more settlers moved west, Native Americans were forced to relocate.

Apache men, women, and children wait in line for food at the San Carlos Reservation.

Explore More!

At first, the U.S. government allowed the Chiricahua Apache to stay on a reservation that included their familiar homeland. Then, they were forced to move. The U.S. government relocated them to the San Carlos Reservation in Arizona with other Apache groups.

TRICKED AND CAPTURED

In 1874, around 4,000 Apache were forced to move to the San Carlos Reservation. It was a harsh, or very unpleasant, place. The land was dry and bad for farming. People were hungry and sick. Sometimes, the food was rotten or filled with worms.

To avoid being sent to the reservation, Geronimo and members of his Apache tribe escaped to Mexico. They then were tricked into thinking they were attending a meeting that would lead to peace. Instead, it was a trap. In 1877, Geronimo was led to the San Carlos Reservation in chains.

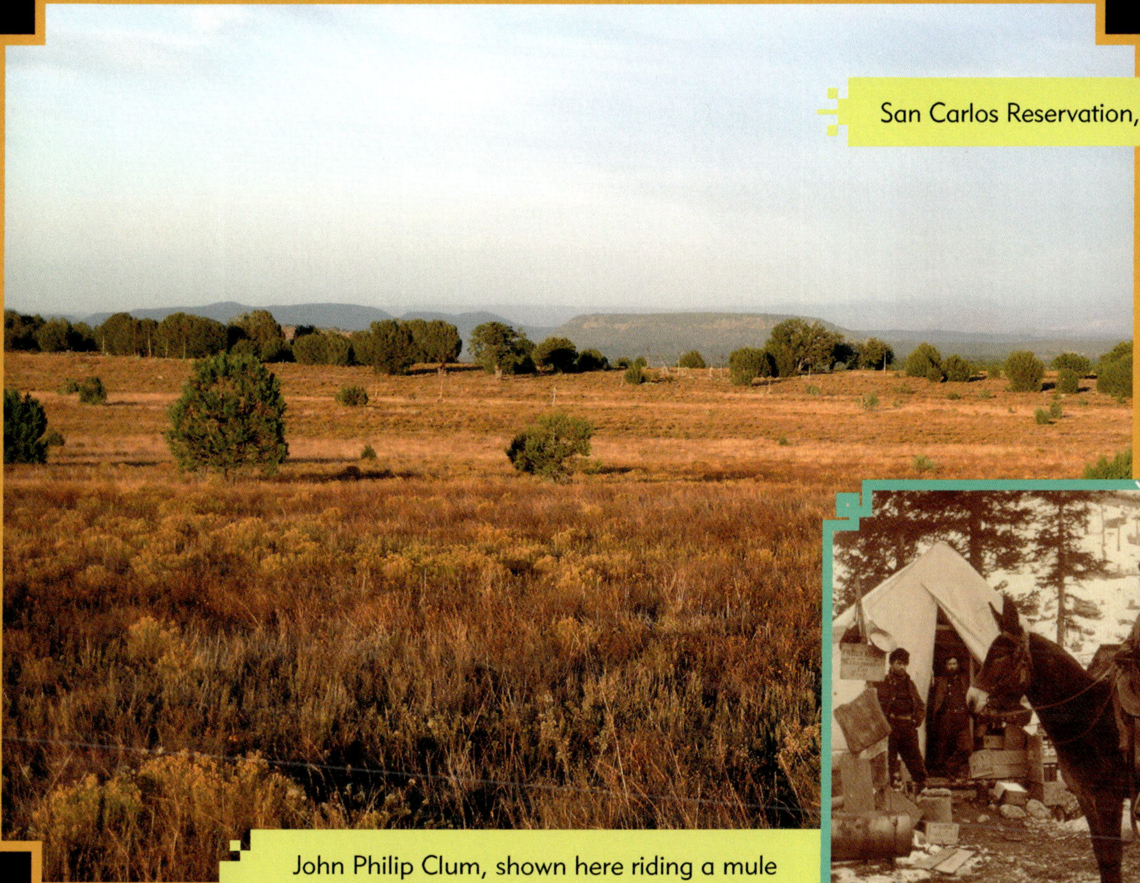

San Carlos Reservation, Arizona

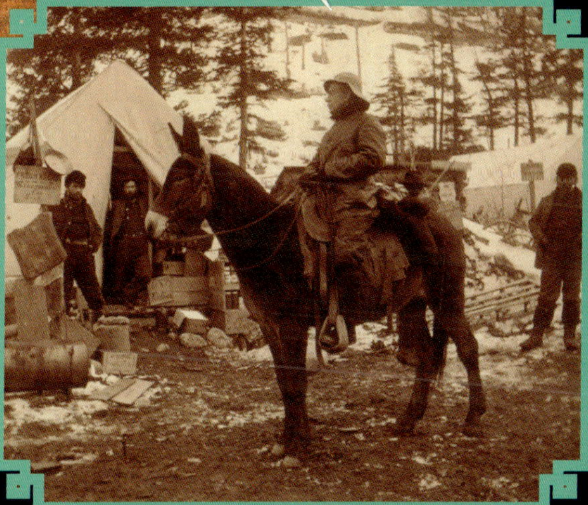

John Philip Clum, shown here riding a mule around 1898, captured Geronimo in 1877.

Over the next 10 years, Geronimo and his followers would escape from the San Carlos Reservation several times. He knew the mountains so well that the U.S. Army had a very hard time finding him. These wild chases made Geronimo famous.

ON THE RUN

Geronimo struggled with life on the reservation. Around 1881, he escaped again. He knew of many hiding spots and was great at avoiding capture. In 1882, the U.S. Army sent in General George F. Crook, who had searched for Geronimo years before.

Geronimo surrendered to Crook in January 1884. Then, Geronimo escaped in May 1885 with more than 130 Apache with him, including many women and children. They surrendered to Crook again in March 1886 near the Mexican border. However, before entering U.S. territory, Geronimo and a small Apache group fled again.

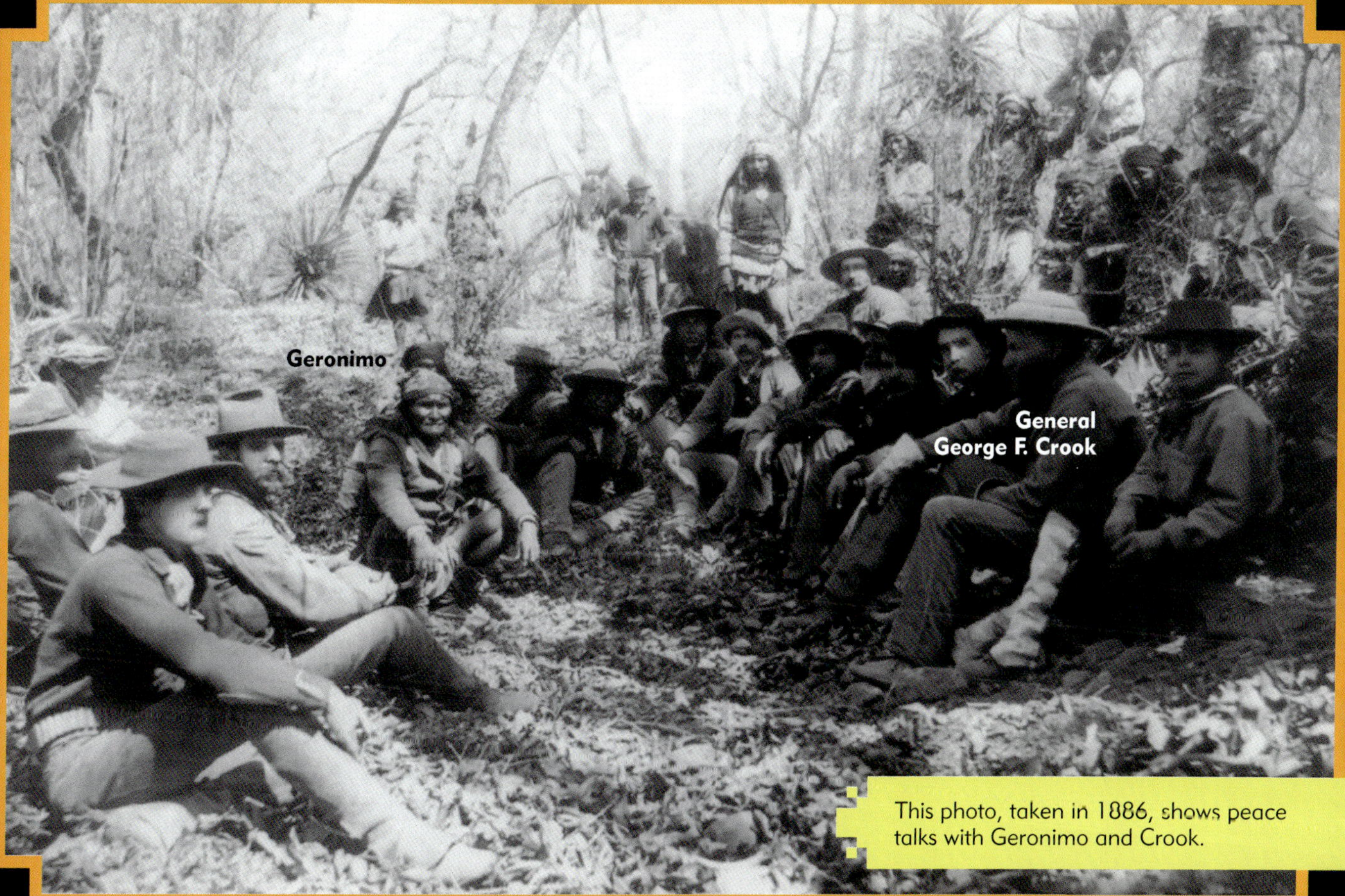
Geronimo
General
George F. Crook

This photo, taken in 1886, shows peace talks with Geronimo and Crook.

Explore More!

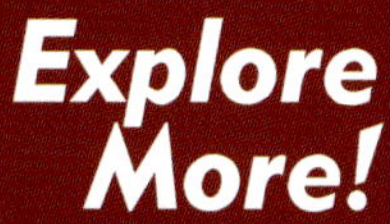

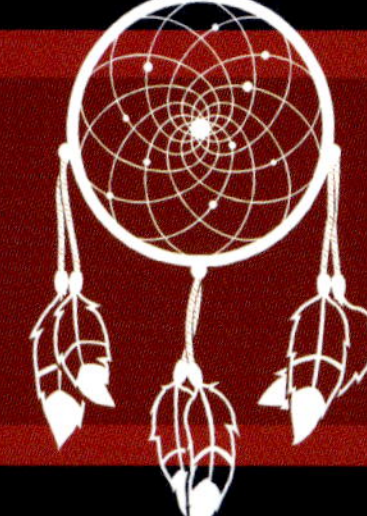

It has been said that Geronimo had a special way of knowing when his band was going to be attacked. This allowed them to move out of harm's way, and it saved many lives. Geronimo was also known as a talented healer.

END OF THE CHASE

The U.S. Army was **determined** to capture Geronimo. They sent Brigadier General Nelson Miles and 5,000 troops to seize him. That was around one-fourth of the whole army! Another 3,000 Mexican soldiers joined in the search.

For five months, Geronimo and his group led the troops on a chase through the mountains. They traveled more than 1,600 miles (2,575 km). Finally, in September 1886, a worn-out Geronimo surrendered to the U.S. government. He only asked that he and his followers could return to their families. The government agreed. Geronimo went peacefully.

Geronimo is pictured here with his camp of Apache in 1886, just before his surrender to General Crook.

Explore More!

Not all Apache people agreed with Geronimo's actions. Some said he was the last great leader of the traditional Apache way of life. Others thought he was a foolish, angry man who was putting the lives of innocent, or blameless, people in danger.

A PRISONER OF WAR

This promise was not kept. On September 8, 1886, the United States shipped Geronimo with 400 other Apache to Florida. They were packed into just 10 train cars. Many became sick and died. Several years later, the nearly starving Apache were moved to Alabama.

In 1894, the Apache, including Geronimo, were then moved to the army base Fort Sill, in modern-day Oklahoma. It was an improvement, but they longed for the Southwest. Geronimo would spend the next about 15 years of his life at Fort Sill. He would never see Arizona again.

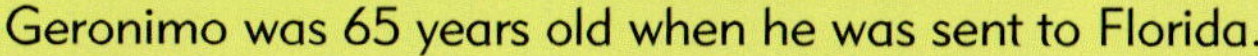

Geronimo was 65 years old when he was sent to Florida.

Geronimo's wife, Ta-ayz-slath, is shown here with their son.

Explore More!

Some facts about Geronimo's life are hard to know for sure. We do know that during his long life, Geronimo had many wives. Different reports say he married six or even nine women. He also was a father to many children.

GETTING FAMOUS

When Geronimo was on the run, he caught the attention of many newspaper writers. In Oklahoma, people often visited him and took photos. He seemed to enjoy posing for the pictures.

By the turn of the century, Geronimo's name was known all over North America. He was even an attraction at the 1904 St. Louis World's Fair. He sold signed pictures of himself for 25 cents. For each picture sold, he was allowed to keep 10 cents for himself. He would also sign and sell items like walking sticks and bows for hunting.

Geronimo (center) stands with other Apache in a show at the 1904 St. Louis World's Fair.

Geronimo drove this Cadillac with other Apache in 1905.

Parade for President Theodore Roosevelt, 1905

Explore More!

In 1905, Geronimo rode in a parade for President Theodore Roosevelt. He met with him to ask if his people could return to their homeland in the Southwest. Roosevelt said no, fearing more violence. The Chiricahua Apache people would not be freed until 1913.

HIS OWN STORY

Geronimo's older years were peaceful. He returned to farming. He became a **Christian**. It is said he felt shame for the killing he had done, above all the blameless individuals. Still, people talked about his brutal, or very violent and severe, actions in battle. Some stories were true, but others were not.

In 1905, the writer S. M. Barrett spoke with Geronimo. Barrett had to get permission to do this, since Geronimo was still a prisoner. The stories were printed in a book, *Geronimo: His Own Story*. The book would keep Geronimo's truth alive for many years to come.

Geronimo with S. M. Barrett and **translator**

Before he died, Geronimo said he wished he hadn't surrendered.

THE LIFE OF GERONIMO

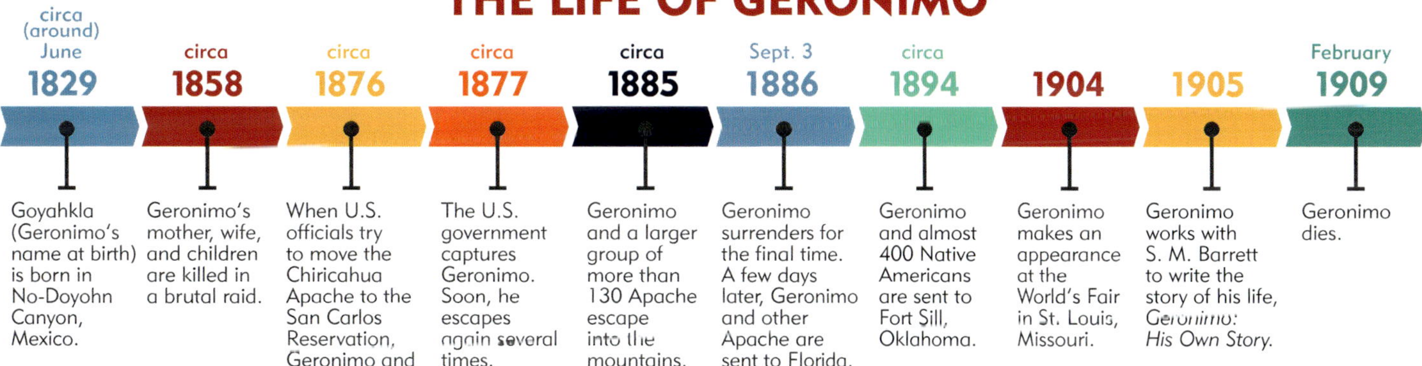

circa (around) June 1829	circa 1858	circa 1876	circa 1877	circa 1885	Sept. 3 1886	circa 1894	1904	1905	February 1909
Goyahkla (Geronimo's name at birth) is born in No-Doyohn Canyon, Mexico.	Geronimo's mother, wife, and children are killed in a brutal raid.	When U.S. officials try to move the Chiricahua Apache to the San Carlos Reservation, Geronimo and others flee.	The U.S. government captures Geronimo. Soon, he escapes again several times.	Geronimo and a larger group of more than 130 Apache escape into the mountains.	Geronimo surrenders for the final time. A few days later, Geronimo and other Apache are sent to Florida.	Geronimo and almost 400 Native Americans are sent to Fort Sill, Oklahoma.	Geronimo makes an appearance at the World's Fair in St. Louis, Missouri.	Geronimo works with S. M. Barrett to write the story of his life, *Geronimo: His Own Story*.	Geronimo dies.

Explore More!

In 1909, Geronimo fell off his horse. He landed in a cold creek and stayed there all night. He was found in the morning, very sick. He died a few days later, reportedly with a family member by his side.

GLOSSARY

Catholic: Someone who is a part of the Roman Catholic Church, which is a Christian faith that the pope leads.

celebrity: A person who is famous.

Christian: Someone who follows the teachings of Jesus Christ.

council: A group of people meant to make decisions for a bigger group.

determined: The powerful feeling of wanting to do something without allowing anything or anyone to get in the way.

Mexican-American War: A war fought between the United States and Mexico from April 1846 to February 1848.

parachute: A specially shaped piece of cloth that collects air to slow something down.

revenge: To harm someone in return for harm done.

traditional: Having to do with long-practiced customs.

translator: One who changes words from one language to another.

violent: Having to do with the use of force to harm someone.

wilderness: A piece of uninhabited land left to grow wild.

FOR MORE INFORMATION

Books

Bird, F. A. *Apache*. Minneapolis, MN: Checkerboard Library, 2021.

Cooke, Tim. *Geronimo*. New York, NY: Gareth Stevens Publishing, 2020.

Sullivan, Laura L. *Geronimo*. New York, NY: Cavendish Square, 2020.

Websites

Biography: Geronimo
ducksters.com/history/native_americans/geronimo.php
Check out more interesting facts about Geronimo here, such as how he described his childhood.

Geronimo
kids.britannica.com/kids/article/Geronimo/353178
Learn the facts about Geronimo on this website just for kids.

Geronimo Facts for Kids
kids.kiddle.co/Geronimo
See photos of Geronimo, including his family, travels, and time in prison.

Publisher's note to educators and parents: Our editors have carefully reviewed these websites to ensure that they are suitable for students. Many websites change frequently, however, and we cannot guarantee that a site's future contents will continue to meet our high standards of quality and educational value. Be advised that students should be closely supervised whenever they access the internet.

INDEX

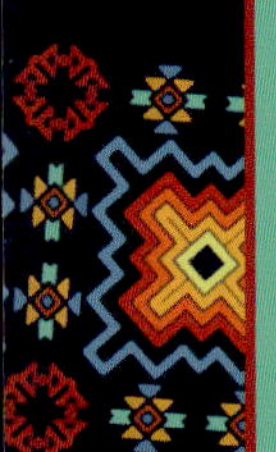